MONSTERS UNCHAINED!

MONSTERS UNCHAINED!

OVER 1,000 DROP-DEAD FUNNY JOKES, RIDDLES, AND POEMS ABOUT SCARY, SLIMY, SLITHERY, SLOBBERY, SPOOKY CREATURES FOR KIDS AND GROAN UPS

RICHARD LEDERER
International Punster of the Year

MARION STREET PRESS
Portland, Oregon

to my mummy and my deady

ACKNOWLEDGMENTS

The vampire limerick on page 18 is by Gary Hallock. The mummy limerick on page 69 is adapted from a version by Tiff Wimberly. The witch limerick on page 87 is by Kirk Miller. The witch limerick on page 89 is adapted from a version by Ken Pinkham.

Thanks to my granddaughters Lucy and Nelly for their suggestions about how to make this book better.

Published by Marion Street Press
4207 SE Woodstock Blvd # 168
Portland, OR 97206-6267
USA
http://www.marionstreetpress.com/

Orders and review copies: (800) 888-4741

Printed in the United States of America
ISBN 9781936863662
Library of Congress Cataloging-in-Publication Data pending

CONTENTS

MONSTERS ON THE LOOSE!

We human beings are fascinated by monsters.

We love reading about monsters. We love playing with monster action figures and dolls. We love watching monsters at the movies and on TV. We love playing monster video games.

Why are we so attracted to monsters?

We are somehow drawn to their ugliness. Monsters are ghastly, grotesque, gruesome, hair-raising, hideous, horrifying, and downright yucky creatures. They are so ugly that their own shadows run away from them. They are so ugly that when they look in a mirror, their reflection looks back and screams. And they are so ugly that when they appear in *Star Wars* movies, they don't wear costumes:

How does a monster count to 25?
   On her fingers.

How does a monster count to 50?
   On her toes.

Who won the beauty contest for monsters?
Nobody.

Why don't monsters remember anything you tell them?
Because what you say will go in one ear and out the others.

FIRST MONSTER MOTHER: "You have the ugliest baby I have ever seen!"

SECOND MONSTER MOTHER: "Thank you very much!"

We humans enjoy the wonderful variety of monsters. The morgue the merrier!:

The Headless Horseman laughed his head off at monster jokes. What kind of horse does he ride?
A night mare.

What do you get when you cross a muscular monster with broccoli?
The Inedible Hulk.

What would you do if you opened your front door and saw Dracula, Frankenstein, a ghost, a ghoul, King Kong, a mummy, a skeleton, a werewolf, a witch, and a zombie standing on your steps?
Hope it's Halloween.

Knock, knock.
Who's there?
Orange.
Orange who?
Orange you glad that you'll be meeting so many monsters?

One, two,

Ghosts go "Boo!"

Three, four,

Zombie gore.

Five, six,

King Kong's tricks.

Seven, eight,

Yetis skate.

Nine, ten,

Werewolf's den.

Eleven, twelve,

Ghouls dig, delve.

Thirteen, fourteen,

Cyclops snorting.

Fifteen, sixteen,

Witch's mix green.

Seventeen, eighteen,

Fiends gyrating.

Nineteen, twenty,

Freaks aplenty.

In spite of their spooky, kooky, and pukey, icky, sticky, and sicky, and hairy, scary, and extra-ordinary appearance, monsters can be very funny:

Why did the monster eat a light bulb?

She wanted a light snack. It really brightened her smile and made her eyes light up.

What is yellow on the outside and red, orange, blue, green, brown, and black on the inside?

A school bus carrying little monsters.

GIRL: "What is big, yellow, and prickly has three eyes, and eats rocks?"

DAD: "I don't know. What?"

GIRL: "A big, yellow, prickly, three-eyed rock eater—and it's crawling up your leg!"

Where do you find monster snails?
On the end of monsters' fingers.

An upside down monster?
How can you tell?
Its nose will run,
And its feet will smell!

And we take monsters very personally:

How do you keep an ugly monster in suspense?
I'll tell you tomorrow!

Where can you see a hideous monster?
Look in the mirror!

What's a monster's favorite food?
You!

In the book you are now reading lurk more than 1,000 monstrous jokes and riddles and 60 poems. These monsterpieces are so weird that they're bound to start showing up on Sickopedia.

The 18 monsters that you're about to meet will lurch through these pages in alphabetical order. That way, from the **A**bominable Snowman to **Z**ombies, you'll always be able to find your favorite freak in his, her, or its own creature feature.

Finally, the Sicktionary at the end of this book provides you with definitions of the hard words.

—Richard Lederer

San Diego, California

richard.lederer@pobox.com

'TWAS HALLOWEEN NIGHT

(thanks to Clement Clark Moore, who wrote "The Night Before Christmas")

'Twas Halloween night, and all through the house,
All the creatures were stirring and eating a mouse.

The monsters had gathered to plan and prepare
For all trick-and-treaters they wanted to scare.

Each creature stepped forth and performed energetically
Their Halloween act and did so alphabetically:

The **A**bominable Snowman, known as a Yeti,
Celebrated the night by tossing confetti.

The **B**ats had a blast, and they left us aghast!
Through the flap in the bat door they flew out so fast.

A **C**yclops awoke, afflicted with pink eye.
In a bad-tempered mood, he gave us the stink eye.

Count **D**racula rose, as he does at night often.
And the whole house was racked by his terrible coffin.

Frankenstein sat bolt upright in his 'lectric chair,
While his bride complained loudly, "I've nothing to wear!"

The **G**hosts were all moaning. Their voices were heated.
They started their meeting with "Let's all be sheeted."

A five-legged **G**houl only mummies could love
Wore polka-dot trousers that fit like a glove.

Godzilla told jokes. Please don't think me a louse:
He wasn't that funny, but he brought down the house.

King Kong climbed the walls and chanted some voodoo.
All over the halls, monkey see, monkey doo doo.

The long **L**och Ness Monster, her eyes rather bleary,
Decided to go for a swim in Lake Eerie.

A chummy old **M**ummy was no crumby dummy.
She dumped treats yummy, gummy down her scummy tummy.

A **S**keleton offered a toast quite upbeat,
Raised a mug of formaldehyde: "Bone appétit!"

A Howl-o-ween **W**erewolf ate garlic that night.
All agreed that his breath was much worse than his bite.

Into the room crept a **W**itch quite inept.
She had just cleaned her house, and the hag overswept.

The **Z**ombies ate eight of St. Nicholas's reindeer.
Then caught Santa Claus and devoured his brain, dear.

All the monsters exclaimed, as they lurched out of sight,
"Happy Haunting to all—and to all a good fright!"

THE ABOMINABLE SNOWMAN

The Abominable Snowman is sweet.
Other monsters he knows how to treat.
He gave Sasquatch one shoe,
E width, size twenty-two,
'Cause Sasquatch is Bigfoot, not Bigfeet!.

Knock, knock.
Who's there?
Abominable.
Abominable who?
A bomb in a bull is dangerous!

Knock, knock.
Who's there?
Snowman.
Snowman who?
Snowman is as ugly as a monster.

The Abominable Snowman, also known as a Yeti, and his wife can be found in the Himalayan Mountains. In fact, Yetis are so big that they're hardly ever lost. Where they live it is so cold that Starbucks serves coffee on a stick. It is so cold that people have to scrape the ice off their glasses! It is so cold that people jump inside their freezers to warm up! It is so cold that Grandpa Abominable's teeth are chattering—in the glass!

The Abominable family is Santa Claustrophobic because they live in an icicle built for two. The chilled-ren call their dad Frozen Pop and Popsicle. Mr. and Mrs. Abominable start the chilled-ren's day with Frosted Flakes and cold cream of wheat and advise them:

- "When you meet other Yetis, always say, "Have an ice day!"
- "Put on your Abominable snowcaps and snowshoes, or you'll catch your death of cold!"
- "When we're on a road trip, stop asking every five minutes, 'Are we there Yeti?'"
- "Don't ever try kickboxing with Bigfoot!"

The Abominables are a family of ice screamers. They love to belt out songs like "There's Snow Place Like Home for the Holidays!" "Frosty the Snowman," and "Freezer Jolly Good Fellow!," listen to rappers like Ice Cube, Ice-T, and LL Cool J, and watch movies like *The Big Chill*, *Ice Age*, and *Frozen*. Mr. and

Mrs. Abominable go dancing at the snow ball. They write to each other on the Winternet.

The Abominable Snowman eats icebergers, cold cuts, spagh-yeti, and baked Alaska. Sometimes he'll grab a Bigfoot-long sandwich at Yak-in-the-Box. He also likes chili, but it makes him blow hot and cold. And he'll treat himself to a snow cone, a Slushy, or a Monster energy drink. When the Yeti eats and drinks too much, he puts on weight, gets thick to his stomach, and becomes the Abdominal Snowman:

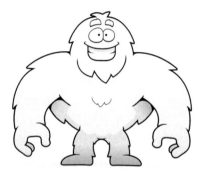

An Abominable Snowman named Matt
Can no longer sit where he sat.
> When he was thin,
> He could sit on a pin,
But now he has gotten too fat!

An Abominable Snowman named Vanya
Tipped over a plate of lasagna.
> And when the poor Yeti
> Spilled a bowl of spaghetti,
He found that the stuff's gooey on ya!

Abominable is ready to hop on his snow mobile or his b-icicle or his slay to go chill out with other yetis, but then he gets cold feet. He doesn't get invited to many parties because he often sticks his Bigfoot in his mouth, Yeti still hangs out with his friends. When they give him the cold shoulder and make him cool his heels, he blows his cool and goes brrrserk!

Now it's time to break the ice. I'm willing Tibet that this snow job of cool Abominable Snowman jokes doesn't leave you ice-olated and out in the cold:

What do you call it when the Abominable Snowman, Dracula, Frankenstein, and the Mummy play golf together?
> *A fearsome foursome.*

How do Yetis keep their pants from falling down?
> *They use snow belts.*

What is big and hairy and bounces up and down?
> *The Abominable Snowman bungee jumping.*

What's white and black and blue?
> *A Yeti who's fallen down a mountainside.*

What happened when the Abominable Snowman recently voted for a Democratic president?

He became known as the Obama-nimble Snowman.

When Sasquatch moved to another mountain, the Abominable Snowman had some big shoes to fill.

What is three feet long and has a tongue and sixteen eyes?

Bigfoot's sneakers.

Where does the Abominable Snowman keep his money?

In a snow bank.

What do you get when you cross the Abominable Snowman with Dracula?

Frostbite.

What do you get when you cross the Abominable Snowman with a witch?

A cold spell.

What do you get when you cross the Abominable Snowman with an octopus and a kangaroo?

A white fur coat with eight sleeves and deep pockets.

What do you get when you cross a Yeti with a dwarf from Oz?

The Abominable Munchkin.

What do you get when you cross the Abominable Snowman with Godzilla?

A jumbo yeti.

What do you get when you cross the Abominable Snowman with a bat?

Cold and flew symptoms.

The Abominable Snowman
Met a slow man
Going to the fair.

The Yeti had fun
Because only one
Of those two men got there!

favorite vegetable: Sasquash.

favorite salad: cold slaw.

favorite toppings: Cool Whip and cool ranch.

favorite fairy tales: The Blizzard of Oz and *Yak and the Beanstalk.*

favorite poet: Robert Frost.

favorite novel: War and Frozen P's.

favorite sport: ice shockey.

favorite hockey team: the Colorado Avalanche.

favorite entertainment: the Ice Follies.

favorite holiday figure: the Nor'Easter Bunny.

favorite countries: Iceland and Chile.

favorite letters in the alphabet: IC ("icy"). *C* turns *old* into *cold* and *hilly* into *chilly.* Also *S* and *F. S* turns *now* into *snow* and *lush* into *slush. F* turns *lakes* into *flakes* and *rigid* into *frigid.*

BATS

A vampire who took long vacations
Planned to visit a number of nations.
When told, with regrets,
That he couldn't take pets,
He replied, "Bats are my blood relations!"

Knock, knock.
Who's there?
Bat.
Bat who?
Bat you a dollar that you haven't heard the jokes in this book.

Bats are fly-by-night operators with lots of hangups. They hang upside down so that they can drop off to sleep.

As little bats grow up, they play bat's cradle and battycake and learn the alphabat so that they can read books like *The Bat in the Hat*. Bats hang down with each other and marry when they fall heels-over-head in love.

Many bats work with witches because many witches are old bats. One witch contracted a skin disease from her pet. She went from bat to warts. Another witch learned poetry from her pet. She went from bat to verse. As one bat said to a witch's hat, "You go on a head. I'll hang around for a while!"

Don't cave when you read these batty jokes. As one bat said to the other, "Time's fun when you're having flies!":

What's brown, has wings, and sticks to the roof of your mouth?
A peanut butter and bat sandwich.

What has 18 wings and catches flies?
A bat baseball team.

Why did the other kids have to let the vampire play baseball?
It was his bat.

Why did the witches' team lose the baseball game?
Their bats flew away.

Why was night baseball started?
Because bats like to sleep in the daytime.

Why can't you ever talk to bats on the telephone?
Because they always hang up.

What floats in the ocean, but only at night?

A bat buoy.

What's the difference between a one-wingéd bat and a two-wingéd bat?

It's a matter of a pinion.

What did the mouse say when she first saw a bat?

"I think I've just seen an angel!"

What does a little vampire call his Egyptian mother and flying mammal father?

Mummy and Batty.

What has mold and flies?

A spoiled bat.

What has wings but can't fly?

A dead bat.

Flutter, flutter, little bat.
How I wonder where you're at.
You fly through the air with the greatest of ease.
You're a brave acro-bat on a flying trapeze!
Flutter, flutter, little bat.
How I wonder where you're at!

Hickory dickory dock.
A bat flew into a clock.
The clock struck one
And then was done.
It nevermore went tick tock!

How do girl bats attract boy bats?

They bat their lashes.

What do you get when you cross a vampire bat with a werewolf?

Whatever it is, the fur would fly.

What do you get when you cross an infant bat with a skeleton?

Baby bat ribs.

What do you get when you cross a vampire bat, a mummy, and a porcupine?

A flying Band-Aid with built-in air holes.

Bat's all, folks!

favorite foods: wings and flapjack batter.

favorite sport: batminton.

favorite game: batgammon.

favorite musical group: the Beatles.

favorite decomposer: Bat-hoven.

favorite superhero: Batman.

favorite part of New York: the Battery.

favorite letters in the alphabet: B and *F*. B turns *at* into *bat,* and *F* turns *lap* into *flap, light* into *flight,* and *lying* into *flying.*

THE BOOGEYMAN

On a cold winter night in a blizzard,
A boogeyman dined with a wizard.
    The café they rode to
    Was all out of toad stew,
So they had to eat raw lizard gizzard.

Knock, knock.
Who's there?
Boogeyman.
Boogeyman who?
Boogey, man, until the sun comes up!

Once upon a slime, a boogeyman shambled into the world. His house is located at the dead end, in a petrified dreadwood forest.

The Boogeyman is very scary. The best way to call him is . . . long distance! The best way to address him is . . . very politely—and from a long way off! What steps should you take if you see the Boogeyman charging you? The longest steps possible! What do you get when you see the Boogeyman? Out of the way! What phone number should you dial when you see a boogeyman lurching your way? 9-Run-Run!

Run, run, run,
As fast as you can.
I'll still catch you!
I'm the Boogeyman!

With fiends like this, who needs enemies? The Boogeyman's motto is "I'm ready, villain, and able." Sometimes you can find this monster boogie boarding. Sometimes you can find him on the dance floor, where he loves to boogie. Other times you can find him sitting on the end of your finger. Then he wonders, "Why is everybody always picking on me?" If you think that's funny, well, it's snot!

Why did the Boogeyman cross the road?
    To scare the kids on the other side.

How do you make a purple boogeyman?
    You cross a red boogeyman with a blue one.

What happened to the boogeyman's kids after they ate all their vegetables?

They gruesome.

What kind of boogeyman has the best hearing?

The eeriest.

Can you tell me how long boogeymen should be fed?

The same as short boogeymen.

What time would it be if five boogeymen were chasing after you?

Five after one.

Which boogeyman has its eyes closest together?

The smallest boogeyman.

How do you make a boogeyman float?

You mix two scoops of ice cream, a glass of soda water, and a boogeyman.

I can't lift a boogeyman with one hand because I can't find a one-armed boogeyman.

What do you call a huge, ugly, slobbering, boogeyman wearing earphones?

Anything you like. He can't hear you.

What do you call a boogey-man with no legs?

Anything you like. He can't catch you.

A boogeyman and a werewolf went out together to see a movie. During the show, the werewolf fell asleep and slumped down in her seat. When the film ended, the boogeyman absentmindedly started to walk out of the theater, but an usher told him, "You can't leave that lyin' around here!"

Responded the boogeyman: "That's not a lion. That's a werewolf!"

favorite foods: hamboogers, fettuccini Afraid-o, scream of wheat, scarrots, creep suzettes, and terror-misu.

favorite candy bar: Baby Ruthless.

favorite drink: demonade.

favorite children's book: The Pukey Little Puppy.

favorite poem: "The Fright Before Christmas."

favorite section of the newspaper: the horrorscope.

favorite actor: Robert Dreadford.

favorite amusement park rides: the scare-o-sel and the scary-go-round.

favorite musical: My Fear Lady.

favorite game show host: Drew Scary.

favorite vice president: Al Gore.

favorite appliance: the scare conditioner.

favorite university: Villainova.

favorite day of the week: Frightday.

favorite letter in the alphabet: S. It turns *care* into *scare*, *car* into *scar*, *cream* into *scream*, *hock* into *shock*, *lime* into *slime*, *lay* into *slay*, and *laughter* into *slaughter.*

CYCLOPS

On a blind date, two Cyclops said, "Hi!"
"You're the ONE EYE adore," they did sigh.
   Now they're married for years,
   And the secret appears
To be that they see eye to eye!

Knock knock.
Who's there?
Eyelash out.
Eyelash out who?
"Eyelash out at any monster that threatens me!" said the Cyclops.

Knock, knock.
Who's there?
Eyesore.
Eyesore who?
Eyesore do like Cyclops jokes.

Knock, knock.
Who's there?
Eyewash.
Eyewash who?
Eyewash I knew more Cyclops jokes.

Have you ever read about a monster with one eye? Actually, you'll do much better if you try reading with both your eyes.

That way, you can read about Cyclops, an ancient Greek monster with one eye in the middle of his forehead. In other words, he has 20 vision. He's a very popular monster because his story is a real eye opener. The eye has it!

Mr. and Mrs. Cyclops ride around on their motor-Cyclops and eye cycle, when they aren't on the blink. They sing to each other, "I only have eye for you!" and "You're the apple of my eye!" They constantly call each other on their eye phones. They eat eye scream together. They toast each other over eyeballs. They go to movies to watch films shown in Eye Max in 1-D. They travel abroad and visit the Eye Full Tower. Then they take a red-eye flight home.

Mr. and Mrs. Cyclops each keep an eye on their kids and read them "Winkin', Blinkin', and Nod." Cyclops moms and dads offer their sons and daughters advice that they hope will be optimistic, not misty optic:

- "Don't ever read in dim light. It will strain your eye."
- "Carry Visene with you at all times. Otherwise, you'll be a total eyesore."
- "Don't ever pretend to be a pirate. When you put the eye patch on, you won't be able to see anything."
- "Don't you ever play with a unicorn. That's just an accident waiting to happen!"

Mr. Cyclops became a teacher, but the principal had to let him go because he had only one pupil. Another problem with being a Cyclops is that people can't tell if a Cyclops is winking at them or just blinking. But the advantage that a Cyclops has is that he never gets cross-eyed! And he can buy glasses at half price!

What do you call a Cyclops hermit?

A private eye.

What does a mean Cyclops give you?

The evil eye.

Why did the girl Cyclops break up with her steady date?

He had an eye for other girls.

When a Cyclops is admitted to the hospital, where is she placed?

In the Eye See You.

There was a little guy
Who had a little eye
Right in the middle of his forehead.
When he was good,
He was very, very good,
But when he was bad, he was horrid!

Little Jack Horner
Sat in the corner
Eating a Christmas pie.
He put in his pinkie
And pulled out a stinky
Old Cyclops that had just one eye!

So now you've read about a monster with one eye named Cyclops. One day you'll find out what the other eye was called.

favorite children's games: peek-a-boo! eye see you! and seesaw.

favorite cartoon character: Popeye.

favorite flower: the iris.

favorite eyewear: monocle.

favorite pet: a seeing eye dog.

favorite icon: the CBS eye.

favorite tsar: Eye-van the Terrible.

favorite letters in the alphabet: *C* and *I—see* and *eye*. Also *E, B,* and *L. E* turns *yes* into *eyes*, *B* turns *row* into *brow*, and *L* turns *ash* into *lash*.

DRACULA

Without fangs you'll hear vampires complain,
"Hey, this sucks!" but I'd like to explain:
If they can't make you bleed,
They will never succeed,
And their biting will all be in vein!

Knock, knock.
Who's there?
Discount.
Discount who?
Discount is named Dracula!

Knock, knock.
Who's there?
Achoo.
Achoo who?
"Achoo on people's necks!" boasted Dracula.

Knock, knock.
Who's there?
Ivan.
Ivan who?
Ivan to drink your blood.

Long ago, vampires sailed to the United States in blood vessels and set up their own monstro-cities and terror-tories. Some settled in the Vampire State, some in New Fangland, and others went west and became batboys for the Colorado Rockies' Horror Picture Show. Other vampires joined the Mafia and became fangsters. Still others moonlighted at night school, while still others attended law school, where they learned how to suck blood during the day, as well as at night.

The most famous of all vampires is Count Dracula, the notorious neck romancer—a real blood count. He lives at 1600 Transylvania Avenue, and every day, the Count receives fang mail from members of his worldwide fang club.

Vampire parents start their kids' days with Shrouded Wheat and Count Chocula, especially when they come in bite-size. When Dracula was a little bat, his count father and countess mother gave him sound advice:

- "Whatever else you do, NEVER run with a wooden stake in your hands."
- "When somebody gives you a compliment, always say, 'Fang you!'"
- "Stop opening the can of tomato juice with your fangs and sucking all the jelly out of the jelly donuts."
- "Study hard for your blood tests at night school, or you'll never graduate Phi Bat-a Cape-a."

- "Always be scareful. Before flew season, make sure you get a blood shot."
- "Drink your soup before it clots."
- "Always bite the hand that feeds you."
- "Don't ever bite your lip."
- "Don't cry over spilled blood."
- "Don't act like a spoiled bat and drive us batty!"

Dracula once fell in love with the girl necks door. She was six feet tall, and Dracula loves to suck up to women. Dracula is a speed demon and owns a Batmobile and bloodmobile, which he refuels at aghast-ation. He loves taking the ladies out in the Batmobile or the bloodmobile and driving like a bat out of heck along major arteries.

But Count Dracula remains a bat-chelor. Whenever he tries to kiss one of his girlfriends, they yell, "Ouch!" Anytime he courts another vampire, he gets under her skin and they end up at each other's throats fighting tooth and nail. Dracula is a real pain in the neck, and drain in the neck, who drives women batty. Every one of his girlfriends has to tell him, "Sorry, you're not my blood type. I'm O positive!"

> You're a woman from East Transylvania
> Dating Dracula, with his weird mania.
> He asks you each night
> To go out for a bite—
> An experience certain to drain ya.

He isn't a very attractive fellow, mainly because he can't see himself in the bat room mirror and so is unable to brush his teeth, comb his hair, take a blood bath in his bat tub, or tie his bat tie. This causes bat breath and the disease Dracula fears most—fang decay.

The fiend went to the dentist to cure his fang-ache and correct his bite. The dentist had to use his vampliers, and the Count ended up with false fangs, which for him are new-fang-led devices that, like Dracula himself, come out at night. All he wants for Christmas is his two front fangs.

Dracula finds his victims in any neck of the woods. He searches for the ones that are the most suck-ulent. If the police question him, the count simply explains that he is a law-a-biting citizen. He hopes that his victims won't cross him and that the cops won't set up a stake-out.

> The maker doesn't want me.
> The buyer doesn't use me.
> The user doesn't see me.
> What am I?
> I am a coffin!

What's the best thing to put on Dracula's coffin? A very tight lid. Dracula lives in a coffin because the rent is so low. He loves the deep plots and grave setting of a cemetery, especially when the temperature rises above 90 degrees. That's when the Count applies SPF80 moon tan lotion and sighs, "There's nothing like a cold bier on a hot day!"

Fangs very much for reading this bleeding-edge history of Dracula. Vampire jokes suck. They totally bite. Nonetheless, I'm going to stick my neck out with some humor you can really sink your teeth into:

What did the waitress ask Dracula?

"How would you like your stake, and do you want cream in your coffin?"

What did the Dracula do when he saw a funeral procession?

He took a turn for the hearse.

What will Dracula do when he dies?

He'll bite the dust.

What does Dracula take for a sore throat?

Coffin drops.

Why was Dracula expelled from school?

For failing the blood test.

How does Dracula feel after sucking blood from a duck?
Down in the mouth.

What did the math teacher ask the vampire to do?
Count, Dracula.

VAMPIRE TEACHER: "How do you spell *coffin*?"
YOUNG DRACULA: "K-A-U-G-H-E-N."
VAMPIRE TEACHER: "That's the worst coffin spell I have ever heard!"

Vampires enjoy going to the casketeria for a quick bite. If they really crave fast food, they go after victims with high blood pressure.

How many vampires does it take to change a light bulb?
None. Vampires prefer the dark.

Why do vampires like to drink blood?
So they won't have to recycle empty bottles.

Or, as Dracula said to his apprentice, "We could do with some new blood around here."

Don't ever play ping pong with King Kong.
Don't ever take blood tests with Dracula.
Don't you dare give a wedgie to Frankenstein.
Your ending will be quite spectaculah!

Don't you dare snap a towel at Godzilla.
Such a prank would be foolishly rude.
Don't you dare floss the teeth of a werewolf.
You are liable to end up as food!

Don't you dare give a hotfoot to Bigfoot.
Don't point a stake at a vampire.
Don't you dare roast marshmallows with dragons.
You'll find you are playing with fire!

Don't you steal witches' brooms for spring cleaning.
Don't ever try scaring a ghost.
Don't ever eat breakfast with zombies.
You'll certainly end up as toast!

Dracula doesn't like to be crossed, but he often is, as the following curious clonings will show:

What do you get when you cross Dracula with a nerd?

Count Dorkula.

What do you get when you cross Dracula with Sleeping Beauty?

Tired blood.

What do you get when you cross Dracula with a manicurist?

A nail biter.

What do you get when you cross Dracula with a chef?

Count Spatula.

What do you get when you cross Dracula and a duck?

Count Quackula or Count Drakeula.

What do you get when you cross Dracula with a witch?

Sweepstakes.

What do you get when you cross Dracula with Long John Silver?

You get a vampirate.

What do you get when you cross a Dracula with a munchkin?

A monster that sucks blood out of your knees.

What do you get when you cross a vampire with a large antlered animal?

Vamoose!

Georgie Porgie, pudding and pie,
Bit the girls and made them die!
When the boys came out to play,
Georgie Porgie flew away!

Little Tommy Tucker
Bit people for his supper.
Then he drank their blood
As a super picker upper!

Vampire Jack went up the hill
To fetch a pail of blood.
Jack fell down and broke his crown.
They buried him in the mud!

Why did Dracula run out of the Italian restaurant?
The chef put garlic on his pizza.

What did Dracula say then he saw a giraffe for the first time?
"I'd like to get to gnaw you. Where do I start?"

What were Dracula's last words?
"No! I said I wanted a steak, not a stake!"

What's the difference between an optimist and a vampire hunter?
One counts his blessings, and the other blesses his counts.

Did you hear about the poor vampire hunter?
He tried to kill a vampire by driving a pork chop through its heart because steaks were too expensive.

A well-mannered vampire from Wheeling
Was endowed with such delicate feeling.
When he read on the door,
"Don't spit on the floor,"
He flew up, and he spat on the ceiling!

Now it's time to say goodbye to Dracula and his batty friends: "So long, suckers!"

favorite foods: fangfurters, littleneck clams, cape-on, suck-atash, alpha-bat soup, blood oranges, and blood pudding.

favorite fruits: Adam's apples and necktarines.

favorite candy: an all-day sucker.

favorite drinks: cold bier, de-coffin-ated coffee with scream, and a bloody Mary.

favorite coffee: Maxwell House. It's good to the last drop! Dracula takes his coffee black. He hopes that it will keep him up all night.

favorite songs: "You're So Vein," "I'm Screaming of a Bite Christmas," and "Auld Fang Sine."

favorite movie: The Vampire Strikes Back.

favorite book: The Vampire Diaries.

favorite children's book: Goodnight Moon.

favorite magazine: Bleeders Die-gest. It has great circulation.

favorite articles of clothing: necktie and neckerchief.

favorite building: the Vampire State Building.

favorite electronic device: blood cell phone.

favorite brand of facial tissue: Kleen-necks.

favorite dog: bloodhound.

favorite dances: the fang-dango and the vaults.

favorite sport: casketball.

favorite activity in art class: drawing blood.

favorite circus act: the jugglers.

favorite holiday: Fangsgiving.

favorite vacation spots: Fanghai, Great Neck, Long Island, and the North and South Poles. There's no sun there for six months of the year.

favorite letter in the alphabet: D. It changes *rink* into *drink* and *rain* into *drain.*

DRAGONS

A dragon with fiery plume
Crashed a wedding and smashed up the room.
Ate every hors d'oeuvre.
Crushed the cake. What a nerve!
Then toasted the bride and the groom!

Knock knock.
Who's there?
Dragon.
Dragon who?
Dragon out a bunch of dragon jokes is a lot of fun!

A brave knight carefully plotted how he would slay a dragon and then marry the king's daughter. Unfortunately, after he confronted the beast, all his plans went up in smoke. That's because dragons are full of hot air. Where there's smoke, there's fire—and dragons have a flare for smoking people.

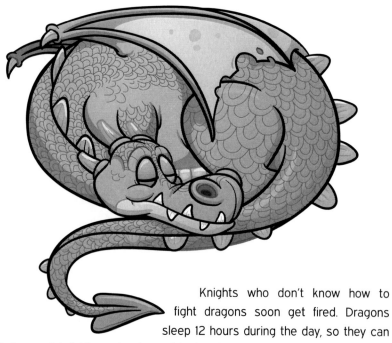

Knights who don't know how to fight dragons soon get fired. Dragons sleep 12 hours during the day, so they can let off steam at knights and enjoy a late-knight snack. Dragons go to church on Sundays, so they can prey on weak knights. That's why knights refer to dragons as "fire hazards" and dragons refer to knights in armor as "canned food." That's why many a knight's tombstone reads, "Rust in Peace."

A dragon once barbecued Lancelot
And instantly started to dance a lot.
Then it smoked Galahad
And thought that was sooo rad.
That dragon had ants in its pants a lot!

After they give up smoking for good, dragons that set the world on fire during their extinguished careers end up in the Hall of Flame. The most famous dragon in the Hall is Queen Elizardbreath!

How do dragons maintain their oral health?
By gargoyling twice a day.

How can you help a dragon lose 30 pounds of ugly fat?
Cut off its head.

Did you hear about the nearsighted woman with insomnia?
She counts dragons instead of sheep.

Why shouldn't you grab a dragon by the tail?
If you grab the end of it, it could be the end of you.

A dragon that lost its tail
In a leaf shredder started to roar.
So where did it go for a new one?
It went to the re-tail store!

Why are dragons so clumsy on the dance floor?
They have two left feet.

What material does a dragon use on the floor of her cave?
Rep-tiles.

What did the dentist shout when she looked into the dragon's mouth?
"Fire in the hole!"

What do you get when you cross a vampire with a dragon?
Count Dragula.

What do you get when you cross an octopus with a dragon?
An octagon.

How can you keep a dragon from charging?
Take away its credit card.

Why do dinosaurs live longer than dragons?
Because they don't smoke.

Why did the dragon visit Miss Muffet?
To find out what the heck a tuffet was.

> Little Miss Muffet
> Sat on a tuffet
> Eating her curds and whey.
> Along came a dragon.
> Its tail started waggin'.
> The two are fast friends to this day.

What kind of tree did the knight turn into after facing a dragon?
Ash.

What did the traffic officer say to the dragon that exceeded the speed limit?
"Where's the fire?"

What's the difference between a knight and Rudolph the Red Nosed Reindeer?
One slays the dragon, and the other's draggin' the sleigh.

How do you make a dragon stew?
Throw a bucket of water at its mouth.

How do you make a dragon fly?
First, you get a huge zipper . . .

favorite foods: baked beings, terror-fried chicken, and hot tamale with hot sauce.

favorite flower: snapdragon.

favorite insects: dragonfly and firefly.

favorite songs: "Baby, Won't You Light My Fire?" "Great Balls of Fire!" "Hot Hot Hot," "There'll be a Hot Time in the Old Town Tonight," and "Smoke Gets in Your Eyes."

favorite folk song: "Puff the Magic Dragon."

favorite book: The Lizard of Oz.

favorite comic book hero: the Human Torch.

favorite game: Dungeons & Dragons.

favorite bird: the flaming-o.

favorite mountains: volcanoes.

favorite sports teams: the Calgary Flames, Miami Heat, and Toronto Raptors.

favorite reading device: Kindle.

favorite brand of tire: Firestone.

favorite letters in the alphabet: F and *S. F* turns *lame* into *flame* and *ire* into *fire*, and *S* turns *team* into *steam.*

FRANKENSTEIN'S MONSTER

Frankenstein wasn't very compliant.
He was mad and annoyed and defiant.
But he happened to pass
Anger management class—
And turned into The Jolly Green Giant!

Knock, knock.
Who's there?
Frankenstein.
Frankenstein who?
Frank 'n' stein is my favorite sandwich and drink.

Doctor Victor Frankenstein was the world's first body builder. He created his monster because he liked to make new friends. For his groundbreaking work he was awarded a Nobel Pieces Prize.

Victor Frankenstein employed a band of headhunters to gather body parts to make monsters. They would chop up corpses and place the pieces in boxes with the label "Some Assembly Required." That way the doctor had his work cut out for him.

The mad scientist wondered if his monster needed a brain like a hole in the head. Doctor Frankenstein had half a mind to make his monster with nothing inside his head, but that would have been a no-brainer. Instead, Victor Frankenstein picked his monster's brain because he liked to change people's minds and give them piece of mind. So, using a dead bolt, he made sure that his creation had a good head on his shoulders.

Despite his evil reputation, Doctor Frankenstein actually had a good sense of humor. He always kept his monster in stitches, because he believed that "a stitch in slime saves nine." When Frankenstein's monster asked the doctor if he could sew himself up, the mad scientist replied, "Sure, suture self!" That made the monster knit his brow, and like two curtains, he ultimately pulled himself together.

When Frankenstein's monster was struck by lightning, it was like a bolt from the blue. The fiend screamed, "Aw shocks! I get such a charge out this! It's just watt I need! I'm a live wire!" When the brute rose from the table and spat on the ground, the proud doctor exclaimed, "It's saliva! It's saliva!" That was an electrifying moment—when the monster met his maker.

The monster had a tough time in junior high school. His classmates teased him about his green complexion and dorky wardrobe. They told him that he looked like death warmed over. They taunted him with a cruel song:

Frankie is a friend of mine.
His full name is Frankenstein.
When he lurches down the street,
We can smell his filthy feet!

Never-ending is this rhyme:
For a nickel or a dime
(Twenty cents for overtime),
He'll belly flop in sticky slime.

Whenever Frankenstein sent his picture to a Lonely Hearts Club, they wrote back and said, sorry, nobody here is that lonely! Whenever a girl ghoul was attracted to Frankenstein, he developed a crush on her and gave her a choker. When she became his main squeeze, that was the end of her. That's why they called him a ladykiller.

Frankenstein's monster had his heart in the right place. In fact, he once had a ghoul friend. He just couldn't resistor. He told her, "Frank-ly, I love you a whole watt! You've stolen my heart! I'm Igor to go out with you! Please be my valenstein!" He also dated a lady scarecrow but went from rags to witches. She was his last straw. Alas, Frankenstein's romantic relationships don't last very long because the nut screws around and then bolts.

When Doctor Victor Frankenstein ran out of corpses, he had an out-of-bodies experience. So he found a new job at a body shop as parts manager.

Sensitive fellow that old Zipperneck was, he developed an identity crisis. The monster kept hoping that he had a mummy and deady, but he was never able to dig them up. So he went to a psychiatrist to see if he had a screw loose and if his head wasn't screwed on right. "I'm at loose ends. I'm coming apart at the seams," he complained to the psychiatrist. "I seem to be going around in circles."

Said the doctor, "That's because somebody has nailed your foot to the floor!"

When the villagers chased Frankenstein's monster, he shrieked at them, "Do you want a piece of me?" When they asked the monster, "Who do you think you are?" he shouted, "Tom, Dick, Harry, Rodney, George, Bruce, Jose, ..." Ultimately, the townspeople came to love Frankenstein's monster. In fact, they were all choked up. They carried a torch for him.

When the Frankenstein was finally buried, the monster's tombstone read, "Rest in Pieces."

DR. FRANKENSTEIN: "This morning I crossed my monster with a piano."

DRACULA: "And what did you get?"

DR. FRANKENSTEIN: "A Frankensteinway. I also crossed my monster with a sponge."

DRACULA: "And what did you get?"

DR. FRANKENSTEIN: "A shock absorber. I also crossed my monster with a penguin."

DRACULA: "And what did you get?"

DR. FRANKENSTEIN: "A creature whose tuxedo is too tight. I also crossed my monster with a frog."

DRACULA: "And what did you get?"

DR. FRANKENSTEIN: "Whatever it turns out to be, you'll be disappointed when you kiss it."

A loony doctor's weird intention
Made a freak of dark dimension.
The mention of his scarred invention
Created tension, deep dissension.

Frankenstein got struck by lightning,
Terror in the village heightening.
Throats of villagers were tightening,
Nothing brightening, all so frightening,

Stitched-up brutes are so insulting,
Unexpected, stressful, jolting.
They generate shock sooo re-volt-ing
That panicked villagers are bolt-ing.

What did Frankenstein say when he saw his neighbor's new car?

"I'm green with envy!"

What does Frankenstein use to go fishing for electric eels?

A lightning rod.

What's red and white on the outside and green and lumpy on the inside?

A can of Cream of Frankenstein soup.

What do you do with a green monster?

Wait until it ripens.

What does the sign read on Frankenstein's office door?

"Out to crunch."

Why does Frankenstein hate flying?

Because every time he goes to the airport, his nuts and bolts set off the alarm.

Why is Frankenstein such a good gardener?

Because he has a green thumb.

FRANKENSTEIN'S MOTHER: "My son's at medical school."

DRACULA'S MOTHER: "What's he studying?"

FRANKENSTEIN'S MOTHER: "Nothing. They're studying him!"

Frankenstein's monster he sat on a wall.
Frankenstein's monster had a great fall.
All the king's horses and all the king's men
Couldn't sew the body parts together again!

How do you keep Frankenstein from biting his nails?

Give him some nuts, bolts, and screws instead.

How did Frankenstein eat his lunch?

He bolted it down.

How did Frankenstein win the election?

He got all the volts.

Why can't Frankenstein finish running a marathon?

He always gets a stitch in his side.

What do you call a brilliant monster?

Frank Einstein.

What monster flies his kite in a rain storm?

Benjamin Frankenstein.

What monster plays the most April Fool's jokes?

Prankenstein.

What's big and green and goes, "Oink, oink"?

Frankenswine.

favorite foods: Frankenfurter, strangled eggs, artery-chokes, and greens. These items have a long shelf life and no expiration date. They're already dead.

favorite cereal: Captain Crunch.

favorite drinks: Jolt and a screwdriver.

favorite aftershave lotion: Brute.

favorite shampoo: Head & Shoulders.

favorite children's game: corpse and grave robbers.

favorite actor: Boris Karloff.

favorite musical: Little Shock of Horrors.

favorite short story: "Turn of the Screw."

favorite music: shock and soul.

favorite singer: Carmen Electricity.

favorite songs: "Put on a Happy Face" and "I Fall to Pieces."

favorite national anthem: "The Scar Strangled Banner."

favorite dog: a black Lab mix.

favor insect: lightning bug.

favorite TV network: Spike.

favorite track star: Usain Bolt.

favorite college bas-ketball team: Wichita State Shockers.

favorite credit card: Master Charge.

favorite football team: San Diego Chargers.

favorite WNBA team: Tampa Bay Lightning.

favorite letter in the alpha-bet: F. It turns *ear* into *fear* and *right* into *fright.*

GHOSTS

A ghost and a witch with a broom
And a ghoul and a bat in a room
Stayed up very late
So that they could debate
About who should be frightened of whom!

Knock, knock.
Who's there?
Boo!
Boo who?
Don't cry. You're about to laugh at some ghostly jokes!

At the spirited Halloween ball the ghosts had a wail of a time. They danced sheet to sheet and boo-gied to some haunting melodies that the band played from sheet music. They loved to eat, drink, and be scary.

Ghosts are undercover agents of terror. At the party, one of the ghosts dressed up in a badly torn sheet. He was a holy terror. Another came in a starched sheet. She wanted to scare people stiff. The ghostly children came dressed up in white pillowcases.

Baby ghosts wear boo-ties and are often sent to dayscare centers and noisery schools, where they sing songs like "Boo boo, black sheet" and read books like *Winnie the Boo*. Little ghosts start their moanings with Ghost Toasties and Fearios, sprinkled with boo-buries.

Little boy ghosts love to play hide and shriek and to short-sheet each other. Little girl ghosts prefer to play with their haunted doll houses, which they decorate with shudders.

Ghost mothers advise their kids:

- "Don't spook until you're spooken to."
- "Boo unto others as you would have them boo unto you."
- "Don't pick the boo-gers in your nose."
- "Before going out, be sure to put your boos and shocks on."
- "Don't forget to sit in the boo-ster seat and boo-ckle your sheet belt. That way, you'll avoid getting boo-boos."
- "Remember to say, 'How do you boo, sir or madam.'"
- "Eat your food without goblin it."
- "Always do your gnome work."
- "If you don't obey me, you'll have to ghost stand in the corner—in the living room!"

Ghosts live in ghost towns and drive Boo-icks, which they park in their mirages. They pick up their chain mail at the dead letter department in the ghost office. Rich ghosts fly to places like Mali-boo, Ghosta Rica, North and South Scarolina, and Casper, Wyoming, on scareplanes, invented by the Fright Brothers. They go bargain haunting at Bed, Bath and B-E-Y-O-N-D and send ghostcards home.

Now that the ghost is clear, it's time for some spirited puns about ghosts. You have more than a ghost of a chance of coming up with the right answers. Bear in mind that every shroud has a silver lining.

What did the sheet say to the ghost?

"Don't worry. I've got you covered!"

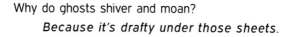

Why do ghosts shiver and moan?

Because it's drafty under those sheets.

What do you call barnyard fowl that haunt your farm-house?

Poultrygeese. And they give you goose bumps.

How can you tell if the chicken coop is haunted?

You keep hearing the poultygeists go "cock-a-doodle-BOO!"

What ghosts play cards?

Pokergeists.

What did one ghost say to the other?

"I don't believe in people."

One ghost said to the other, "You look terrified, as if you've just seen a human!"

Those ghosts—hip! hooray! Hallelujah!
If you're famous, they're bound to pursue ya.
But here's advice sage:
If you sing on their stage,
The audience surely will boo ya!

What did the guard say when a spirit approached the haunted house?

"Halt! Who ghost there?"

What do you call a ghost that haunts the town hall?
A night mayor.

Why don't ghosts like rain?
It dampens their spirits.

Why does an elevator make ghosts happy?
Because it lifts the spirits.

Where do ghosts learn to become pilots?
At fright school.

What's white and serves hors d'oeuvres?
Casper the friendly host.

What's green and can walk through walls?
Casper the friendly pickle.

Did you hear about the girl who wanted to marry a ghost?
Her parents couldn't understand what possessed her.

Did you hear about the ghost who turned to a life of crime?
He was the black sheep of the family.

What happens when a ghost haunts a theater?
The actors get stage fright.

Why do ghosts never get arrested?
The cops can't pin anything on them.

How do ghosts keep in shape?
They exorcise regularly.

What happens when you fire your exorcist?
You get ex-spelled and repossessed.

Why are ghosts in cemeteries so noisy?
Because of all the coffin.

Why was the ghost surprised when his girlfriend showed up for their date at 11 p.m.?
He didn't ex-specter until midnight.

Where do Native American ghosts hang out?
At the Happy Haunting Grounds.

Why did the game warden arrest the ghost?
He didn't have a haunting license.

What do you get when you cross Bambi with a ghost?
Bamboo.

What do you get when you cross fake chocolate with the ghost of an elk?
Carob-boo.

What do you get when you cross a ghost with a cow?
Vanishing cream.

What do you call a ghost who haunts small hotels?
An inn specter.

What do you use to get into a haunted house?
A spook key.

What do you call a ghost that sits in the picture window of a haunted house?
A window shade.

When do ghosts haunt skyscrapers?
When they are in high spirits.

Why did the tiny ghost join the junior high school football squad?
Because he heard that they could use a little team spirit.

What do you call a ghostbuster?
A spooksperson.

How do ghosts fix broken bicycle wheels?
They put in extra spooks.

How do goblins get their books published?
They use ghost writers, who help them meet their deadlines.

What's the title of the book listing well-known ghosts?
Who's Boo.

What do you call a goblin that gets too close to a campfire?

A toasty ghosty.

The sister of Hannibal Lector
Thought there did not exist any specter,
Till a ghost draped with burlap
Sat right down on her lap,
And her panic attack nearly wrecked her!

What do you call a ghost with a wooden leg?

A hobblin' goblin.

What do you call the ghosts of dead turkeys?

Gobblins.

What kind of phone calls do goblins make?

Ghost to ghost.

What happens when a ghost gets lost in the fog?

She is mist.

What do you get when you cross two dogs with a ghost?

A cocker poodle boo.

What disease do ghosts fear the most?

Boobonic plague.

What's the only weight class for boxing ghosts?

Phantomweight.

What's the difference between a monastery and a person wanting to live to 150?

One doesn't have a chance of a ghost, and the other doesn't have a ghost of a chance.

favorite foods: ghost liver pâté, spook-ghetti, fillet of soul, and deviled eggs.

favorite desserts: boo meringue, birthday quake, and Haunted Toll House spookies.

favorite soda: a float.

favorite flower: a boo-quet of mourning gories.

favorite fairy tales: Sleeping Boo-ty and *Boo-ty and the Beast.*

favorite magazine: Good Housecreeping.

favorite amusement ride: the roller ghoster.

favorite toy: the boo-merang.

favorite product: a big scream TV.

favorite TV show: "America's Most Haunted."

favorite daytime talk show host: Phantom of the Oprah.

favorite kinds of music: soul and spirituals.

favorite singer: Awraitha Franklin.

favorite songs: "Ghost Riders in the Sky" and "America the Boo-tiful."

favorite movie: Poltergeist.

favorite painting: the Moaning Lisa.

favorite articles of clothing: a boo tie and boo jeans.

favorite places to shop: boo-tiques.

favorite fictional detective: Sherlock Moans.

favorite branch of the military: the Ghost Guard.

favorite color: boo!

favorite letters in the alpha-bet: G and D. G turns a *host* into a *ghost*, and *D* turns *read* into *dread*.

GHOULS

Tonight, when the last light is gone
And you're sleepy and yawned your last yawn,
    Ghouls and ghosts will come out
    Witches, bats—but don't pout:
All those monsters will leave before dawn.

Knock, knock.
Who's there?
Voodoo.
Voodoo who?
Voodoo you think you're talking to?

Ghouls are 288. Two gross.

A book store clerk said to a ghoul woman, "Here's a good book, *How to Help Your Husband Get Ahead.*"

The ghoul woman answered, "No, thank you. My husband's got two heads already."

You greet that two-headed ghoul by saying, "Hello to you—and to you, too." He was at the top of his class because when a monster puts its two heads together, two heads are better than one. He can literally "watch his head." He also engages in a lot of doubletalk and loves to attend baseball doubleheaders.

One ghoul had eight arms. She was very handy. Another ghoul had no fingers. She was all thumbs. Yet another fiend gave his right arm to become a ghoul, so had only one arm. He overpowered a gang of zombies single handedly—and then he went to the second-hand store, where they lent him a hand. And still another ghoul had only one leg. She worked at I-HOP. Many humans hate ghouls that don't have any feet. That's because those people are sooo lame—and lack-toes intolerant.

A ghoul with six arms and eleven legs walked into a tailor shop. "Quick!" screamed the tailor to his assistant. "Hide the 'Free Alterations' sign!"

After he died, Vincent van Gogh became a ghoul. Somebody talked his ear off. When Captain Kirk, of the starship *Enterprise*, died, he too became a ghoul. Now he has a left ear, a right ear, and a final front ear. Same with that fellow in the coonskin hat who had a single ear growing out of the middle of his face—Davy, Davy Crockett, King of the wild front ear!

Ghouls have names they use for human beings: breakfast, lunch, and dinner!

That's right. Ghouls eat people. That's what keeps ghouls so healthy. Catching people is terrific exercise, and the food is always fresh. Ghouls especially like to eat tightrope walkers because they provide a well-balanced meal. And studies show that eating people boosts the ghouls' dead corpuscle count and hemo-goblin and that all that brain food makes them smarter. Ghouls also shop at health food stores because they find the merchandise there to be super natural.

Knock knock.
Who's there?
Aida.
Aida who?
"Aida lot of people every day," said the ghoul.

Young ghouls read Mother Ghouls nursery rhymes and practice tom-ghoulery by playing games like Swallow the Bleeder.

Their mothers seem to have eyes in the back of their head. No, wait. They actually *do* have eyes in the back of their head—and they offer their little ghouls and boys words of wisdom:

- "Don't be late for dinner, or everyone will already be eaten."
- "Never eat people on an empty stomach. Always eat people on a plate."
- "Remember: A ghoul and his mummy are soon parted."
- "Before you go out in the rain, be sure to put on your ghoul-ashes."
- "Hang out with demons because demons are a ghoul's best friend."
- "Do what I tell you, or you'll end up in deform school!"
- "If you disobey me, it will be over my dead body!"

Eat your heart out over ghoulish jokes. If you don't, a ghoul will:

> On a bright, crystal clear starry night,
> When the full moon was just at its height,
> Romeo met
> His grotesque Ghouliet.
> That's what we call love at first fright!

Why did the ghoul get expelled from school?
He kept buttering up his teachers.

What do ghouls call skateboarders?
Meals on Wheels.

What do you call a 12-year-old monster?
A junior high ghoul student.

What do ghouls do on family picnics in the Forest of Oz?
Munch kin.

Did you hear about the ghoul with six legs?
He won a race by six feet.

Did you hear about the ghoul that looked like something the cat dragged in?
Actually, she WAS something the cat dragged in.

Why didn't the ghoul make new Facebook friends?
She was busy digesting her old Facebook friends.

Yankee Ghoulie went to town,
Riding on a great mare.
He stuck his head in a garbage can,
And this is what he ate there:

Gross, green gobs
Of greasy, grimy goblin guts,
Big, bloody blobs
Of blackened, bulging Bigfoot butts,

Mutilated mutant meat,
Frankenstein's foul, filthy feet—
Eeeew! Munch! Chew! Crunch!
Yankee Ghoulie chowed his lunch!

Why do female ghouls go on diets?
To keep their ghoulish figures.

What do young female ghouls do at parties?
They go around looking for edible bachelors.

Why did the girl ghoul knit herself three socks?
Because she grew another foot.

Why do the ghouls on the women's basketball team never weep after losing games?
Because big ghouls don't cry.

What should a cab driver give a carsick ghoul?
Bus fare.

Why do ghouls like trophies?
Because they are en-graved.

What do you get when you cross a ghoul with a train?
A monster that will choo-choo you up.

What do you call a ghoul that ate his mother's sister?
An aunt eater.

What did the ghoul say to his ghoulfiend?
"Hello, gore juice."

What did the ghoul buy for his ghoulfiend?
A set of his and hearse pajamas.

A ghoul woke up one night in a terrible temper. "Where's my dinner?" he yelled at his wife. "And where are my axe and my chains?"

"Don't bite my head off! Stop being such an ogre!" exclaimed the ghoul's wife. "I've only got four hands!"

What did the ghoul do after she attended charm school?
She continued to eat people—but with a knife and fork.

Why did the ghoul eat a stick of dynamite?
She wanted her hair to grow out in bangs.

favorite foods: Hungarian ghoul ash, handburgers, frank-footers, human beans, tongue, hard boiled legs, cauliflower ears, pickled bunions, ladyfingers, and eyes-cream.

favorite snacks: Ghoul Scout cookies, French ghost, and Butterfingers.

favorite drinks: slime flavored Ghoul-Aid and rot and mold running water.

favorite toppings: Ghoul Whip and grave-y.

favorite songs: "Oh, What a Beautiful Mourning," "Ghouls Just Want to Have Fun!" "Somewhere Ogre the Rainbow," and "I Left Her Heart in San Francisco."

favorite musical instrument: the organ.

favorite movie: The Gizzard of Oz.

favorite book: Ghoulliver's Travels.

favorite bedtime story: Ghoul deWarlocks and the Three Scares.

favorite hockey team: Detroit Deadwings.

favorite hockey position: ghoulie.

favorite bird: the swallow.

favorite flowers: mari-ghouls and morning gories.

favorite holiday: April Ghoul's Day.

favorite TV show: Chomping on the Stars.

favorite letters in the alphabet: ODS DK ("odious decay").

GODZILLA

Titanic, gigantic Godzilla
Stomped on Tokyo, then on Manila.
Then sank a flotilla,
Then fought a gorilla,
And gulped down a vat of vanilla!

Knock knock.
Who's there?
Tyrannosaurus Wrecks.
Tyrannosaurus Wrecks who?
Tyrannosaurus Wrecks Tokyo!

As a modern dinosaur, Godzilla is a colossal fossil. He throws his weight around. He's a larger-than-life mover and shaker. When you talk to Godzilla, you have to use big words. If you greet him with "Hi!" he'll say, "I sure am!" If you ask him, "What's up?" he'll answer, "Me!"

Godzilla is so huge that he has his head in the clouds. He's so monstrous that when he steps on a scale, the dial says, "to be continued." He's so mammoth that he breaks into bowling alleys so that he can use the balls to play marbles. He's so ginormous that his dentist has to climb a ladder to drill the monster's cavities—with a jackhammer! He's so humongous that when he steps on a skunk, he becomes the world's biggest stinker, and he smells to high heaven!

Where does Godzilla travel? Anyplace he wants to! He always knows when he reaches Tokyo. He can feel himself stepping on more people. What can you find between Godzilla's toes? Slow runners.

What time is it when Godzilla sits on your car? Time to buy a new car. Godzilla crushes a lot of cars, turning them into Tyrannosaurus Wrecks. One day, Godzilla stepped on Batman and Robin. The result was Flatman and Ribbon.

What does Godzilla spread on his toast? Traffic jam. Godzilla occasionally eats a china closet, four chairs, and a dining room table. That's because he has a suite tooth. Godzilla thought about eating the Big Ben clock in London, but he decided that the task was too time-consuming. The monster would never devour Athens. It has too much Greece. He would never consume Cardiff because he wants to save Wales. But in late November, Godzilla will eat Turkey.

Of course Godzilla is a cold-blooded killer. He's a reptile, and all reptiles are cold-blooded. But in his favor, he doesn't eat people. That's because he doesn't care for Japanese food.

Godzilla stories are tall tales. Godzilla jokes may be over your head, but they're head and shoulders above all other jokes, and they give you something to look up to:

What do you get when you cross King Kong with a humongous Asian monster?

A Godzilla Gorilla.

What do you get when you cross Godzilla with a kangaroo?

A lot of big potholes in the Tokyo streets.

What do you get when you cross a Godzilla with a witch?

A dino-sorceress, and she would need a pretty big broomstick.

What do you get when you cross Godzilla with another witch?

Tyrannosaurus hex.

What do you get when you cross Godzilla with a witch's black cat?

Whatever it is, I don't want to be the one who cleans its litter box.

What do you get when you cross Godzilla with a parrot?

A lot of big talk.

What do you get when you cross Godzilla with a vampire?

A really big sucker.

What do you get when you cross Godzilla with a munchkin?

A chameleon that crushes ants.

What do you get when you cross Godzilla with a pig?

Jurassic Pork.

What do you get when you cross Godzilla with a termite?

Dinomite.

What do you get when you cross Godzilla with a black cat?

A monster that makes you very nervous when it crosses your path.

FIRST GIRL: "Would you rather have the Godzilla attack you or King Kong?"
SECOND GIRL: "I'd rather that Godzilla attacked King Kong!"

Where does Godzilla go to the bathroom?
> *The dinosewer.*

What do you call Godzilla in a phone booth?
> *Stuck.*

How can you tell Godzilla is in your refrigerator?
> *Look for his footprints in the Jell-O.*

Can King Kong fit in your refrigerator?
> *No. Godzilla's already in there.*

Why should you never play catch with Godzilla?
> *He's very, very heavy, and you'll strain yourself.*

Why did Godzilla return to Tokyo?
> *He wanted to get back to his old stomping grounds.*

What's the best way to raise Godzilla?
> *With a crane.*

Why doesn't Godzilla eat uranium?
> *He's afraid he'll get atomic ache.*

How does Godzilla get to sit in the top of a tree?
> *He sits on an acorn and waits.*

How does Godzilla get down from sitting in the top of a tree?
> *He sits on a leaf and waits for the fall to arrive.*

Why does Godzilla paint his toenails red?
> *So he can hide in cherry trees.*

But I've never seen Godzilla in a cherry tree.
> *See, his camouflage is working.*

How did Tarzan die?
> *Picking cherries.*

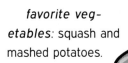

favorite vegetables: squash and mashed potatoes.

favorite appetizer: one ton soup.

favorite drink: Orange Crush.

favorite candy bar: Nestlé's Crunch.

favorite songs: "Sixteen Tons" and "It's a Small World After All."

favorite children's song: "Tokyo Bridges Falling Down."

favorite dance: the Monster Mash.

favorite baseball team: the San Francisco Giants.

favorite animal: the terror-dactyl.

favorite quiz show: Who Wants to be a Godzillionaire.

favorite letters in the alphabet: C and *M. C* turns *rush* into *crush,* and *M* turns *ash* into *mash.*

THE INVISIBLE MAN

> The Invisible Man came to dine.
> He sat right to my left, which was fine.
> But his rumblings abdominal
> Were simply phenomenal—
> And everyone thought they were mine!

Knock, knock.
Who's there?
The Invisible Man—so nobody's there!

What's the difference between the Invisible Man and an honest lawyer? You can't find either one, but the Invisible Man actually exists.

Let's be clear about the Invisible Man because everything about him is clear. In his case, what you don't see is what you get.

Invisible's mother and father are also invisible. They're his transparents. They told his trans-sister and him that children should be heard and not seen. The family owns the Invisible Dog. They have to be very careful where they step on the lawn.

As a child, the Invisible Boy played "Peek-a-boo, I see you! Fiddle dee dee, you can't see me!" In the *Star Wars* films he always rooted for Darth Fader and read every edition of *Where's Waldo*? At school, he would recite the Pledge of Allegiance: ". . . one nation invisible, with liberty and justice for all."

When Invisible was a teenager, he didn't have any friends. There was simply too much disappear pressure, and he wasn't much to look at. Whenever he went to hang out with friends, they'd say, "Long time no see!" But when he tried to make a point with his friends, they'd say, "Who said that?" or "We don't see where you're coming from" or "We can see right through you!" or "You're a Nowhere Man."

The Invisible Man leads a sad life. Like Count Dracula, he can't see himself in the mirror, so he can't groom himself. Not that it matters, because nobody can see him anyway.

Invisible never gets noticed by his friends. He gets terrible grades in school because the teachers keep marking him absent. He can't use social media because there's no picture he can post on Facebook. He can't fly in a plane because he lacks photo I.D. He never wins any honors because he can't get recognized. He receives no medical treatment because the doctor is unable to see him. And everybody can see that he's not all there. They think he's crazy. You know: Out of sight, out of mind.

Jokes about the Invisible Man are simply out of sight! Here they are:

Oh, those jokes were written in invisible ink, but here's a little poem that's worth looking into:

> If you put the Invisible Man
> In a cage in a Monsters Museum,
> The problem will turn out to be
> That no one who comes there can see him!

favorite soup: vanishing cream of mushroom.

favorite drink: evaporated milk.

favorite game: Etch A Sketch. It makes images disappear.

favorite article of clothing: See-Through Panty Hose.

favorite letter of the alphabet: W. It turns *here* into *where*?

KING KONG

A sing-song gorilla is King Kong.
He likes to hear church bells go ding dong!
But when he shakes a steeple,
It scares all the people.
Ever after, those church bells will ring wrong!

We go ape over King Kong. He's grand!
Biggest monarch in all of the land!
You might think he's scary,
But he's tall, dark, and hairy,
And has girls in the palm of his hand!

Knock, knock.
Who's there?
Gorilla.
Gorilla who?
Gorilla cheese sandwich for me, please.

Snatched from Africa, King Kong was thrown in a cage and brought to New York City. When he first saw the Statue of Liberty, he asked her, "Are you my mother?"

King Kong was made to work for peanuts. This made him very angry, and he carried a chimp on his shoulder. The big ape also developed a bad allergy and broke out. Kong then wreaked havoc on New York City. First, he took the five o'clock evening train home—but they made him give it back. Then he ran away with the circus and stole the show, but they made him give that back, too.

King Kong went bananas over Queen Kong. She was his prime mate, the gorilla his dreams. Queen Kong went on a diet to regain her gorilla-ish figure. Then she won a beauty contest and was awarded Beast in Show.

King Kong climbed up the Empire State Building. He tried to take the elevator, but he couldn't fit inside. After scaling the heights of New York's business world, King Kong made it to the top and tried to catch a plane. Alas, he was knocked off the spire of the Empire State Building and made a smash hit on Broadway.

When King Kong fell to his death, he landed on a coal worker and turned him into A flat miner. The gorilla's last words were, "I don't offer any ape-ology for all the damage I've caused. I told you not to monkey around with me!" You can read about Kong's life in John Steinbeck's book *The Apes of Wrath*.

Why don't they include King Kong in animal crackers?
Because he's too big to fit in the box.

What did Dorothy in *The Wizard of Oz* sing to a big ape?
"King Kong, the witch is dead!"

Why does King Kong have such large nostrils?
He has large fingers.

How does King Kong get down the stairs?
He slides down the banana-ster.

What happened when King Kong won a door prize?
He didn't accept it because he already had a door.

What did King Kong say when he heard that his sister was expecting a baby?
"Well, I'll be a monkey's uncle!"

Why did King Kong chase after a werewolf?
He felt like catching some fast food.

How can you tell when King Kong is hiding under your bed?
Your nose is touching the ceiling.

Jingle bells, King Kong smells
A pint-sized Christmas elf.
With a grunt, he eats the runt,
And then he burps himself!

What's the best way to get King Kong to sit up and beg?
First, get a two-ton banana . . . .

What do you get when you cross King Kong with a werewolf?
A howler monkey.

What do you get when you cross King Kong with Donald and Daffy?

Duck Ape.

What do you get when you cross King Kong with a frog?

A gorilla that climbs up the Empire State Building and catches airplanes with its tongue.

What do you get when you cross King Kong with Humpty Dumpty?

A gorilla that climbs up the Empire State Building and lays an egg on Broadway.

What do you get when you cross King Kong with a pigeon?

A lot of very worried New Yorkers.

What do you get when you cross King Kong with a witch's black cat?

A monster that will put YOU out at night.

What do you get when you cross King Kong with a parrot?

A creature that says, "Polly wants a banana—and I want it NOW!"

What do you get when you cross King Kong with a sheep?

A baaa-boon.

What do you get when you cross King Kong with a flower?

A chimp-pansy.

What do you get when you cross King Kong with petroleum?

A grease monkey.

What's the difference between King Kong, a crown prince, and a bald-headed man?

One is a hairy parent, one is an heir apparent, and one has no hair apparent.

What is big, hairy, and flies really fast?

The King Kongcorde.

Why did King Kong join the army?

To learn about gorilla warfare.

favorite cereal: Ape Nut Flakes topped with ape-ricots.

favorite drink: Oranga-Tang.

favorite snacks: chocolate chimp cookies and Rhesus Pieces.

favorite books: Planet of the Apes and *Tarzan of the Apes.*

favorite children's book: Curious George.

favorite cartoon character: Magilla Gorilla.

favorite songs: "Give My Regards to Broadway" and "Jungle Bells, Jungle Bells."

favorite singing group: the Monkees.

favorite area in the playground: the monkey bars.

favorite ruler: Ape-oleon Baboon-aparte.

favorite tool: monkey wrench.

favorite castle: San Simian.

favorite store: Banana Republic.

favorite letters in the alphabet: C and *P. C* turns *limb* into *climb,* and *P* turns *aw* into *paw.*

THE LOCH NESS MONSTER

A monster that took many dips
In Loch Ness grew quite wide in the hips.
It was her sea food diet:
She would see food, then try it.
She especially liked fish and ships!

Knock knock.
Who's there?
Lochs.
Lochs who?
Lochs and bagels are delicious!

The Loch Ness Monster, also known as "Nessie," lives in the inky depths of a lake ("loch") in Scotland. Nessie is apparently female because scientists have determined that the creature is a she-serpent. As a she-serpent, Nessie keeps her lake clean by using a mermaid service.

In a single day Nessie crossed the loch twice, but she never took a bath. That made the monster a dirty double crosser. You'll soon see the Loch Ness Monster in a new movie where she co-stars with a giant shark. It's called *Loch Jaws.*

A little boy asked his mother if he could go swimming in Loch Ness. "Certainly not!" she replied. "You could get kilt doing that."

"But," said the boy, "daddy's swimming in there."

"That's different," said Mother. "He's insured!"

Whenever the Loch Ness Monster meets someone, she says, "Long time no sea!" When she departs, she says, "See you later, navigator!" If you wish to communicate with the Monster, just drop her a line. Nessie may even send you a photograph signed with a water fountain pen.

Loch Ness Monster jokes are not just all wet. They make a big splash. They're deep, but not too deep to fathom. Indeed, these little pieces of humor make for whopping big tails!:

Why did Nessie earn only average grades in school?

Because she is a C monster.

What happened when Nessie's grades starting falling?

They sank below C level.

Why was Nessie dizzy?

Her head was swimming.

Why was Nessie embarrassed?

She accidentally swam into Davy Jones' locker room.

What spooky creature swims and sings this song?:

> Everybody hates me.
> Nobody likes me.
> I'm gonna go and eat worms.
>
> Big, fat juicy worms,
> Little, small skinny worms.
> Golly, how they squirm!
>
> Bite the heads off.
> Suck the juice out.
> Throw the skins away.
>
> Nobody knows
> How I can live
> On sixty worms a day!

The answer is *The Loch Ness Songster.*

What spooky creature has a big claw and a small one and scuttles along the deep, dark ocean floor?

The Loch Ness Lobster.

What do you get when you cross a Scottish locksmith, a bird, and Frankenstein?

The Lock Nest Monster.

What do you call a giant lizard with a stiff neck?

The Locked Neck Monster.

Which monster is the most untidy?

The Loch Mess Monster.

Which monster is the most unfortunate?

The Luck Less Monster.

Where does Nessie look in the newspaper for a job?

The Kelp Wanted section.

What happens to Jewish Loch Ness boy monsters?

They get serpent-cised.

What's the difference between a jumping warlock and a tearful Loch Ness Monster?

One is a leaping wizard, and the other is a weeping lizard.

What's the difference between a Scottish monster and an over-excited trick-and-treater on Halloween?

One is Loch Ness, and the other should knock less.

favorite foods: lox, submarine sandwich, watermelon, water chestnut, and watercress.

favorite books: *Twenty Thousand Leagues Under the Sea, Watership Down, Moby Dick,* and *Hucklebury Finn.*

favorite children's book: *One Fish Two Fish Red Fish Blue Fish.*

favorite song: "Be Kind to Your Web-Footed Friends."

favorite theater: a dive-in movie.

favorite movies: The Little Mermaid, Ocean's Eleven, and *The Codfather.*

favorite paintings: water colors.

favorite piece of furniture: a water bed.

favorite card game: Go Fish.

favorite products: Scotch Tape and scales.

favorite detergent: Tide.

favorite vacation spot: Finland.

favorite letters of the alphabet: H, I, J, K, L, M, N, and *O.* That translates into "*H* to *O*"—"H_2O"!

THE MUMMY

THE MUMMY · 69

The curse of the mummy is true. Some
See her as creepy and gruesome.
       But she'll step out in style,
       Smile and hope all the while
To go out with King Tut as a twosome!

Knock knock.
Who's there?
Egypt.
Egypt who?
Egypt me when he sold me that mummy case but didn't tell me that it came with the original owner.

Movies about the Mummy have drawn huge audiences. Crypt writers create very funny mummy jokes, and the audiences get to watch the action in Horrorscope. Off the silver screen the Mummy isn't very popular with the other monsters. They find him to be all wound up. They think he's egotistical because he's all wrapped up in himself. Ghosts dislike the Mummy because he always tears up their sheets.

That can be explained by the fact that the Mummy was very confused as a child because his daddy was a mummy. When he asked his parents, "Why can't I play with grandmummy?" they replied, "Be quiet! You've already dug her up three times!"

One day, all the Mummy's bandages fell off. He had to stay in the hospital until he was completely recovered.

After that unfortunate incident, the Mummy became chummy with a lady mummy that he met at the county pharaoh. The two mummies had a wedding and tied the knot. For their honeymoon they booked a trip with Club Dead to the Gauza Strip so that the two of them could unwind. They planned for the future by buying a lot of afterlife insurance. After many centuries, the couple turned into moldy oldies, so they decided to retire to the old, old, old age home.

Tomb It May Concern: Here are some mummified riddles and jokes that are quite fresh because they came in Plastic Wrap. Satisfaction guaranteed, or your mummy back!:

A mummy who thought she was dying
Kept crying and crying and crying.
       Until a ghoul said,
       "You're already dead!"
Then that poor mummy's tears started drying.

Why are mummy mommies lucky?

Because they never have to wrap their babies in diapers.

Why did the mummy move out of the pyramid after 1,000 years?

Because she was finally old enough to leave home.

What do mummies wear at Halloween parties?

Masking tape.

Why is it safe to tell mummies your secrets?

They will keep them under wraps because they know that "Mummy's" the word!

Why did the mummy put fabric softener in her bathwater?

To get rid of the static cling.

What did the mummy Superman say to the mummy Lois Lane?

"Shall we sleep in the Kryptonite?"

A talented mummy from Ammon
Said, "I make my dad proud and my mom, and
Though a young whippersnapper,
I'm the world's greatest wrapper.
I play trumpet, and I Toot Uncommon!"

Why are mummies always late?

Because they get all tied up.

Where do mummies go when they feel all tied up?

To the Cairo-practor.

How do mummies send messages to each other?

Through crypt-o-grams.

What do mummy tourists like to do out in the desert?

Peer amid the pyramids.

Why do mummies need to have their homes exterminated?

To drive out the crypt ticks.

Why don't mummies face up to their problems?

Because they live in a state of de-Nile.

What do mummy cheerleaders yell?

"Ra! Ra!"

What did the ancient Egyptian ventriloquist use in his act?

A dummy mummy.

Why did the mummy go to the beach?

To bury herself in the sand.

What do mummies use to groom their feline pets?

Catacombs.

What happened when King Midas touched a mummy?

It became a golden moldy.

What do you get when you cross a mummy with a vampire?

A gift-wrapped bat.

What do you get when you cross a royal mummy with an auto mechanic?

Tut and Car Man.

As the ancient Egyptian said after she had finished preparing the mummy, "That pretty much wraps it up!"

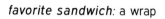

favorite sandwich: a wrap

favorite fruit: poisonbury.

favorite children's stories: Wrapunzel and *Raggedy Ann.*

favorite amusement park: Knots Bury Farm.

favorite flower: chrysanthamummy.

favorite music: ragtime and wrap.

favorite musical group: the Grateful Dead.

favorite quiz show: Name That Tomb!

favorite underwear: Fruit of the Tomb.

favorite parasite: tapeworms.

favorite restaurant: Pizza Tut.

favorite means of transportation: wrap-id transit.

favorite baseball team: Cincinnati Deads.

favorite holiday: Mummy's Day.

favorite letter in the alphabet: T. It turns *error* into *terror.*

SKELETONS

There's a high-spirited skeleton, Nero—
To me, he's a genuine hero.
  But some folks think he's shoddy—
  A gutless no body—
With a body mass index of zero.

Knock knock.
Who's there?
Defeat.
Defeat who?
Defeat bones connected to de ankle bones.

A lot of people say bad things about skeletons. "Get a life!" they taunt. "You're a bonehead, a numbskull, a bag of bones, and a lazybones! You're totally heartless and gutless!"

Cruel people laugh that skeletons are creatures that started diets and forgot to stop. But let's face facts: We are all skeletons wearing skin. So if you want to become a skeleton, go out into the woods at midnight and get so frightened that you jump out of your skin!

Skeletons usually don't go to parties. They don't have any body to dance with. They don't have the stomach for it, and their hearts aren't in it. Moreover, their Facebook pictures are X-rays, which other creatures don't find especially attractive.

When a skeleton does attend a party, she hopes to have a bone-rattling good time and engage in some skull duggery. So she starts by saying to the bartender, "I'll have a pop and a mop!" The other guests try to use her as a coat rack, and the musicians try to play her like a xylophone. But the skeleton stays calm because nothing gets under her skin and it's no skin off her nose.

Mama and papa skeletons offer their children suggestions for a better life:

- "Drink at least 10 glasses of milk a day. It's good for your bones."
- "In winter, wear a warm coat, or the cold will go right through you."
- "Never play with werewolves. They're just after your bones!"
- "If you want a package delivered quickly, use the bony express."
- "Listen to what I tell you! I work my fingers to the bone for you!"

Now it's time to bone up on skeletons with a bone-us of some bone-chilling, rib-tickling, spine-tingling riddles and jokes guaranteed to tickle your funny bone:

What do you use to get into a locked cemetery?

A skeleton key.

Why did the skeleton cross the road?

To get to the body shop.

What do you call a skeleton snake?

A rattler.

What's the scariest job in the world?

The graveyard shift with a skeleton crew.

How did the skeleton know it was going to rain?

She could feel it in her bones.

How did the skeleton woo his girlfriend on Valentine's Day?

He said, "I love every bone in your body!"and gave her bone-bones in a heart-shaped box.

Why can't skeletons play music in church?

They don't have any organs.

Why are skeletons always bone dry?

No sweat.

What do you call a skeleton that is always telling lies?

A bony phony.

What do skeletons do when the electricity goes out in their homes?

They plug their appliances into their eye sockets.

What did the skeleton magician say at the start of her act?

"Abra-cadaver!"

Who was the famous female skeleton who rode naked on a horse?

Lady Cadaver.

Why did the skeleton princess remain unmarried her whole life?

Because her father felt that no male skeleton cadaver.

What do you call a skeleton that doesn't have all his fingers on one hand?

Normal. A skeleton's fingers are divided equally between its two hands.

And as skeletons say to their friends going on cruises, "Bone voyage!"

favorite foods: spare ribs, T-bone steak, baked bones, and skullions.

favorite fish: piranhas. They turn people into skeletons.

favorite salad dressing: Wishbone.

favorite plates: bone china.

favorite place to eat: the cadaver-teria.

favorite song: "I Ain't Got No Body."

favorite musical instrument: trombone.

favorite TV show: Bones.

favorite "Star Trek" character: Bones.

favorite art form: skullpture.

favorite color: bone white.

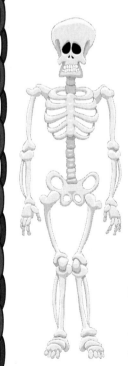

favorite banner: the pirate's flag, a skull and crossbones.

favorite summer sport: skulling.

favorite winter sport: the skeleton.

favorite baseball team: Boston Dead-sox.

favorite vacation spot: Deadwood, South Dakota.

favorite historical figure: Napoleon Bone-apart.

favorite fictional detective: Sherlock Bones, as played by Basil Wrathbone.

best subject in school: Anatomy.

favorite body of water: the Skull Kill River.

favorite letters in the alphabet: B and *M. B* turns *one* into *bone*, and *M* turns *arrow* into *marrow.*

WEREWOLVES

This limerick isn't a stretch.
It's about an unfortunate wretch.
 A werewolf pursued him.
 How did he elude him?
He threw it a stick and
yelled, "Fetch!"

Knock, knock.
Who's there?
Hair comb.
Hair comb who?
Hair comb a pack of werewolves.

Did you know that as soon as they are born, werewolves eat the stork that delivered them? These creatures have an odd number of parents—one maw and four paws. Werewolf dads aren't very good about taking care of werewolf babies. They only change when there's a full moon out.

Werewolf mothers, on the other paw, share their wisdom teeth with their werecubs:

- "Always be polite. When you meet a human being, say, 'Pleased to eat you.'"
- "Don't speak with your mouth full of people."
- "Don't wolf your meals. Play with your food before you eat it."
- "Be sure to tell me if you get a stomachache. It could be someone you ate."
- "Be sure to eat a lot of sheep. That way, you can floss and dine at the same time."
- "Don't go to the zoo when there's a full moon. They might not let you out."
- "When you go to bed, be sure that the jackal lantern night light stays on."
- "Don't use the toilet as a punch bowl."

Werewolves sure love Howl-o-ween—
The best howliday they've ever seen.
How could werewolves ask for more?
The treats show up at their front door!
And when the kids shout, "Trick or treat!"
That's when the werewolves lick and eat!

A man turned into a dark alley—and then he turned into a werewolf. "I'm just not myself today," he complained. His friends replied, "You are really something else!"

The bright-eyed and bushy-tailed werewolf moved to Howlywood, where he auditioned for bit parts. He ended with a role he could really sink his teeth into. The movie was a comedy, and he had the audience howling with laughter.

The werewolf sweated a lot in a heavy fur coat, so he had to visit the Laundromat almost every day. He became a washin' werewolf. Then he became a pastor and said to his congregation, "Let us prey." After that, he became an animal rights activist and started wearing fake fur. Finally, he took up clay-spinning and became a hairy potter.

That's the tooth, the whole tooth, and nothing but the tooth. Now, just fur fun, hair are some hair-raising riddles and jokes about werewolves:

> A man begged, "Doc, please take my case.
> "I think I'm a werewolf! How base!"
> The doctor first sighed,
> And then she replied,
> "Have a seat, please, but first comb your face!"

What do you call a dentist who cleans a werewolf's teeth?
Crazy.

What happened to the werewolf who brushed his teeth with gunpowder?
He kept shooting his big mouth off.

Why are werewolves hairy?
Because if they had feathers, they'd be werechickens.

How can you get fur from a werewolf?
Run fast in the opposite direction and get as fur away as possible.

> I know a werewolf, name of Finnegan.
> He grew whiskers on his chinnegan.
> Along came the wind and blew them in again.
> Poor old werewolf Finnegan. Begin again.

Why did the werewolf cross the road?
So he could eat the chicken.

A werewolf limped into an old western saloon and snarled, "I'm looking for the man who shot my paw!"

How do you tell a good werewolf from a bad one?
If it's a good werewolf, you will be around to talk about it later.

What has thick brown fur and flies?
A dead werewolf.

What's brown on the outside and hairy on the inside?
A werewolf inside a paper bag.

What sleeps four feet up in the air?
A werewolf on its back.

What has four legs and one arm?
A happy werewolf.

Why did the werewolf cross the road?
To get to the other's hide.

Knock, knock
Who's there?
Howl.
Howl who?
Howl you be dressing up for Halloween?

What game do you play with a smelly werewolf?
Hide and reek.

Where do werewolves live?
In werehouses.

Why was the werewolf angry with the skeleton?
He had a bone to pick with him. (Actually 206 bones!)

What did the werewolf say to the skeleton?
"It's been nice gnawing you."

Why did the werewolf say to the grand piano?
"Your teeth are so straight and clean!"

Werewolves sleep like a babies. Every two hours they wake up and howl.

What happened to the werewolf who lived in a tiny apartment?
He developed clawstrophobia.

Two werewolves named Larry and Mary
Had a furry cute baby, not scary.
But what should they dub
Their adorable cub?
Is it Tom? Is it Dick? Is it Hairy?

WEREWOLF MOTHER: "If you were a good father, you'd take Junior to the zoo."

WEREWOLF FATHER: "Why should I? If the zoo wants him, let them come and get him!"

Why was the werewolf arrested in a butcher shop?

She was caught chop-lifting.

What was the name of the film about a werewolf that swam underwater?

Claws.

What werewolf visits you on Christmas Eve?

Santa Claws.

What does a werewolf get when walking on the beach at Christmastime?

Sandy claws.

What's the disadvantage of being a female werewolf?

The all-over perms are very expensive.

What happened to the werewolf that swallowed a clock?

She got ticks.

In his teenage years, who did the werewolf composer Mozart hang out with?

A Wolfgang.

Two men were walking in the woods when they heard the horrible howl of a werewolf, and it sounded very nearby.

The first fellow immediately sat down of a log and began lacing up his running shoes. The second fellow asked, "Why are you doing that? There's no way that you can outrun a werewolf."

"I don't have to outrun the werewolf," answered the first man. "I just have to outrun *you!*"

What wears a thick coat in the winter and pants in the summer?

A werewolf.

Why can't you sneak up on a werewolf?

Because he's an aware wolf.

What do you call a lost hairy monster?

A wherewolf.

What do you get when you cross Bugs Bunny with a hairy monster?

A harewolf.

What do you get when you cross Smoky with a hairy monster?

A bearwolf.

Name some cousins of werewolves.

Whatwolves, whenwolves, and whywolves.

What do you get when you cross Dracula with a hairy monster?

A bloodhound or a Big Bat Wolf whose bite is worse than his bark.

What do you get when you cross a werewolf with a vampire?

A fur collar that fangs around your neck.

What do you get when you cross a werewolf with a rooster?

An animal that howls when the sun rises and goes "cock-a-doodle-doo" at night.

What do you get when you cross a werewolf with your pet dog?

A terrified postman.

What do you get when you cross a werewolf with a sheep?

Something that's wild and woolly.

What do you get when you cross a werewolf with a goat?

You have to get a new goat.

What do you get when you cross a lumberjack with a hairy monster?

A timber wolf.

Knock, knock.

Who's there?

Decry.

Decry who?

Decry of de werewolf sends shivers up my spine.

WOMAN: "Where can I find some fleas?"

WEREWOLF: "Search me."

What's the difference between a werewolf and a comma?

A werewolf has claws at the end of its paws, and a comma is a pause at the end of a clause.

What's the difference between a mangy werewolf and a dead stinging insect?

One is a seedy beast, and the other is a bee deceased.

How did the werewolf feel about devouring Little Red Riding Hood?

He was gladiator.

What do you call a metric werewolf?

The liter of the pack.

What do you call a hairy monster wearing a wool sweater?

A wolf in sheep's clothing.

Where does a werewolf file her claws?

Under the letter "C."

How does a werewolf sign her letters?

"Best vicious."

> Old Mother Hubbard
> Went to the cupboard
> To get her pet werewolf a bone.
> But when she got there,
> The cupboard was bare,
> So the werewolf ate up the old crone!

> Hey diddle, diddle, the cat took a piddle
> All over the werewolf's fur.
> The wolf didn't think that it was fun.
> And puked all over her!

favorite children's game: peek-a-boo. I bite you!

favorite novel: Call of the Wild.

favorite hairy tail: Where the Wild Things Are.

favorite hairy tail character: the Big Bad Wolf.

favorite comic strip characters: Lucy and Linus Van Pelt.

favorite gaming system: Prey Station.

favorite movies: The Wolf of Wall Street and *Predator.*

favorite TV series: Claw & Odor.

favorite TV newscaster: Wolf Blitzer.

favorite basketball team: the Minnesota Timberwolves.

favorite piece of classical music: "Peter and the Werewolf."

favorite musical: Hair!

favorite songs: "Howl, Howl, the Fang's All Hair!" "By the Light of the Silvery Moon," and "Moonlight Becomes You."

favorite music group: The Beastie Boys.

favorite vacation spot: Tombstone, Hairizona.

favorite hotel: the Howliday Inn.

favorite organization: Wolf Cub Scouts.

favorite branch of the military: the Hairforce.

favorite letters in the alphabet: B. It turns *east* into *beast. C.* It turns *law* into *claw. H.* It turns *air* into *hair* and *owl* into *howl. T.* It turns *ail* into *tail.*

WITCHES

A witch burnt her butt on a candle.
She was angry. It was such a scandal.
She jumped on her broom
And zoomed to her doom.
Went too fast, so she flew off the handle!

Knock, knock.
Who's there?
Witch.
Witch who?
Witch way to the haunted house?

Knock, knock.
Who's there?
Witch.
Witch who?
Gesundheit!

Witches are flying sorcerers. They drink their tea out of flying saucers.

When they're in a rush, they get on the stick—the broomstick, that is. On Halloween night, they hop on their brooms and sweep through the air. They prefer to ride brooms because vacuum cleaners are too heavy, and the electric cord isn't long enough.

Witches tell time on their Timehex and Rolhex witch watches. While in flight, they tie their witch watches to their broomsticks. Then you can hear the brooms tick. When a flying witch breaks the sound barrier, you can hear the broom boom and turn into a vroom stick.

Witches' faces look like a million dollars, all green and wrinkly. Witches actually hire out their faces as a cure for hiccups. Their husbands take them to work because they don't want to kiss them goodbye.

Witches think they're funny because every time they look in the mirror, it cracks up. Their hair hangs down to their waist—from under their armpits. Witches are so ugly that when a witch baby is born, the doctor slaps her mother. The baby's parents don't throw a party; they throw up.

But witches take good care of their little baby broomers. They feed them a lot of healthy magic formula in the morning and sing lullabies to help the little tykes go to sweep. They serve them Lucky Charms and Rice Kreepies, because Rice Kreepies go Snap! Cackle! and Pop!

Little witches stir strange ingredients in soup bowls and fly around on whisk brooms. Adult witches and warlocks offer the kids a frothy brew of wisdom and counsel:

- "Study hard for your hexaminations, especially in spelling."
- "If you are sitting in a bathroom stall next to one occupied by a mummy, do not use its bandages as toilet paper!"
- "Please don't ask for the keys to the broom more than once a week."
- "Don't be a road hag. If your broom goes out of control and breaks, you'll have to witch-hike."

> A witches' hotel treats each guest
> With something that leaves them impressed.
> If you call, they will zoom
> Right on up to your room.
> Their broom service is simply the best!

Many witches end up on radio; they have the perfect face for it. If they want to appear on television, they make themselves attractive and bewitching by dieting with Weight Witches, going to the ugly parlor and the scare dresser, and applying scare spray and mass-scare-a. They often become weather witches because they're so good at forecasting. The more charming ones end up appearing on "Lifestyles of the Witch and Famous."

One witch became a movie star. She teamed with a werewolf in the famous film *Ugly and the Beast*, directed by Stephen Spellberg. Another witch had the face of a beauty queen, but she had to give it back.

One year Halloween was visited by a humongous storm. It was raining black cats and bloodhounds! On that Halloween night, a witch went trick-or-treating and collecting goodies in her wicked basket. For her costume, she draped herself with several strings of blinking Christmas tree bulbs. She was a lights witch.

Now is the witching hour, a time for witchful thinking. Here is a bubbly cauldron of black magic jokes about witches:

How many witches does it take to change a light bulb?
Just one—and she changes it into a rabbit.

Why did the witch cross the road?
To get to the dark side.

What happened when the little witch misbehaved at school?
She was ex-spelled.

What contests do witches always win?
The ugly pageants.

When the witch said, "Abracadabra," nothing happened. She was a hopeless speller. But a witch named Wanda was terrific at casting spells. She was a magic Wanda.

Knock, knock.
Who's there?
Wanda.
Wanda who?
Wanda go for a ride on a witch's broomstick?

Double, double, toil and trouble.
Fire burn and cauldron bubble.
Eye of Cyclops, werewolf's claw.
Hunchback's hump and King Kong's paw.
Horseman's head and Hulk's green thumb.
Marinate in ghoul drool scum.
Dragon scales and zombie's ears.
Pour in a vial of ghostly tears.
Mummy's rags and wing of bat.
Tail of warty witch's cat.
Vampire's fang and Bigfoot's fur.
Give the yucky mix a stir!

I will eat it all with glee—
If it has no broccoli!
I'll swallow all, with happy shouts—
As long as there's no Brussels sprouts!

What did the witch name her cooking pot?
It was called Ron.

What do witches call their garages?
Broom closets.

What do Australian witches ride on?
Broomerangs.

Why are witches like candles?
They're both wick-ed.

Why do witches use pencil sharpeners?
To keep their hats pointy and their broomsticks cutting edge.

Why do witches wear pointy hats?
To fit their pointy heads.

Why don't witches wear flat hats?
Because there's no point to them, so the witches look like dorks.

Did you hear about the witch who made it big in major league baseball?
Every day, she practiced her pitchcraft.

Did you hear about the witch who was born with an upside-down nose?
Every time she sneezed her hat blew off.

Did you hear about the witch who gave up fortune telling?
She couldn't see any future in it.

When the young witch tries so hard to hex ya,
She messes it up and just wrecks ya.
Her words just don't gel.
She simply can't spell,
'Cause she suffers from witchcraft dyslexia.

Did you hear about the witch who sprinkles poison on people's corn flakes?
She's a cereal killer.

What do you call a cowardly old hag who lives at the beach?
A chicken sand witch.

What do you call a bunch of blushing sorceresses?
An embarrassment of witches.

How do you make a witch scratch?

Take away the "w."

Why did the twin witches wear name tags?

So that everyone could tell which witch was which.

What is the motto of witches?

"I came! I saw! I conjured!"

Why didn't the witch change the toad into a handsome prince?

Because she preferred kissing a toad.

Why can't a witch sing well?

She has a frog in her throat.

> If you meet a witch in a bog,
> On a rock or a stump or a log,
> It really is better
> That you don't upset her.
> She might turn you into a frog!

What flies on a broom and carries a medicine bag?

A witch doctor.

FIRST WITCH: "I can make an animal drop from the clouds."
SECOND WITCH: "What animal are you talking about?"
FIRST WITCH: "Rain, dear!"

What do you get when you cross a witch with an insect?

A spelling bee.

What do you get when you cross a witch with Mickey Mouse?

Disney spells.

What's the difference between a deer and a small witch?

One is a hunted stag, and the other is a stunted hag.

What's the difference between the store where humans shop and the one where witches shop?

One is a Wal-Mart, and the other is a Mall-Wart.

What do you call an insect witch?

A coven-ant.

What kind of telephone calls do witches make?

Poison to poison.

What do you call a magic snake that keeps witches away from your house?

A witch shield viper.

What do you call a witch's purse?

A hag bag.

What do you call a nervous witch?

A twitch.

What do you call two witches who live together?

Broommates.

Who do witches get good bargains?

Because they like to hag-gle.

What has six legs and flies?

A witch and her cat riding together on a broom stick.

Why did the witch send her broom to the dry cleaner?

She wanted a clean sweep.

What happened when the witch's pet fell off her broomstick?

It was a cat-astrophe.

What do you get when you cross a witch's cat with a canary?

A peeping tom.

What do you get when you cross a witch's cat with a lemon?

A sour puss.

What do you get when you cross a mute owl with a witch?

A creature that doesn't give a hoot about being ugly.

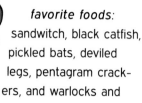

favorite foods: sandwitch, black catfish, pickled bats, deviled legs, pentagram crackers, and warlocks and bagel with scream cheese.

favorite dessert: devil's food cake.

favorite drinks: apple spider and witch hazelnut coffee.

favorite cartoon characters: Broomhilda, The Wizard of Id, and Wand-a Woman.

favorite fairy tale: Sleeping Ugly.

favorite fairy tale character: The Wicked Witch of the West.

favorite music: hagtime.

favorite songs: "It's Not Easy Being Green," "We're Off to See the Wizard," and "Help Me, Wand-a."

favorite game: tug of warlock.

favorite movie series: Star Warts and *Star Warlocks.*

favorite piece of jewelry: charm bracelets.

favorite product: a computer with a spell checker.

favorite automobile: a Ford Hocus Focus.

favorite fictional detective: Warlock Holmes.

favorite recreation: black arts and witchcrafts.

favorite school subject: spelling.

favorite vacation spot: Witch-ita, Kansas, and Green Witch, Connecticut.

favorite group of colleges: the poison Ivy League.

favorite animal: the Tasmanian devil.

favorite letters in the alphabet: pressed *O* ("presto!"). Also *W* and *B*. *W* changes *itch* into *witch, and* into *wand,* and *art* into *wart. B* changes *room* into *broom.*

ZOMBIES

An innocent fellow named Tim
Met a zombie quite horrid and grim.
    Tim patted its head
    Before it had fed.
I wonder what happened to him!

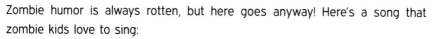

Knock, knock.
Who's there?
Zombies.
Zombies who?
Zombies make honey and zombies don't.

Zombie humor is always rotten, but here goes anyway! Here's a song that zombie kids love to sing:

> The worms crawl in, and the worms crawl out.
> Your eyes fall in, and your teeth fall out
> Into your stomach and out your mouth.
> And your brains come tumbling down your snout.
>
> Worms eat your eyes, and they eat your nose.
> They eat the gook between your toes.
> They eat your intestines and scramble your heart.
> You feel like you are falling apart.
>
> The worms that crawl in are lean and thin.
> The worms that crawl out are fat and stout.
> They eat your heart out, eat your germs—
> Those eeewy, gooey, chewy worms!

Have you ever been to a zombie party? They'll invite anybody they can dig up. They're absolutely dying to meet you, and they especially love brainy boys and girls. One zombie asked a bartender, "Would you please make me a Zombie?" The bartender answered, "It looks like somebody already has!"

Zombies speak Latin because it's a dead language. Zombies aren't very good artists, but they sure can draw flies. Zombies can't carry a tomb or make beautiful music, but they're great at decomposing.

Zombies act crazy because they have lost their minds. Zombies are in grave condition. They are always dead on their feet. Just before Halloween, zombies love eating the brains out of the center of pumpkins.

Zombie children start their day by eating Raisin Brain and Dreaded Wheat. Zombie parents pass on grave guidance to their little ones:

- "Don't bite off more human flesh than you can chew."
- "Never eat people with your fingers. Your fingers should be eaten separately."
- "Stop biting your fingernails, or we'll have to cut off your hands!"
- "When the waiter asks if you want a French, Russian, or Italian dressing on your salad, ask for all three of those people."
- "Whenever you want to have friends over for dinner, we'll be delighted to serve them."
- "Listen to what we say, or we'll ground you—very deeply!"
- "Do what we tell you or you'll be the death of us!"

What goes "ha ha ha ha bonk"? A zombie laughing her head off. That zombie should have quit while she was a head. Being a zombie can get expensive. It can cost an arm and a leg. If that arm and leg were on the left side of the zombie's body, he'll be all right. One zombie entered a lawsuit in court even though her case was so lame that she didn't have a leg to stand on. She hoped that the judge would give her a life sentence.

At ate o'clock, zombie families go to an All-You-Can-Eat restaurant—and eat all the customers. Or they go to KFC and lick other people's fingers. Or they go to reducing salons and chew the fat.

Actually, zombies seldom go out to restaurants because once they've eaten the waiter, there's nobody left to serve them. When zombies go on a diet, they only eat children. As soon as they get their teeth cleaned, they eat the dentist. One zombie ate both her parents and threw herself on the mercy of the court as an orphan. Another zombie swallowed eight people, and then burped 7-Up. When he was offered more food, he said, "No thanks. I couldn't eat another mortal!"

A husband zombie and a wife zombie caught a man from Hungary and another from Czechoslovakia and ate them. When the police captured the two zombies, they x-rayed them, hoping to find the missing men. The X-rays showed that the Hungarian's remains were in the bulging belly of the zombie wife—and the Czech was in the male!

But there are some people that zombies find hard to swallow. They don't eat clowns because clowns taste funny. They don't eat track stars because track stars give them the runs. And they don't eat missionaries because it's hard to keep a good man down. I hope that jokes like these don't leave a bad taste in your mouth:

What's black and white and dead all over?
A zombie wearing a tuxedo.

Why did the zombie cross the road?
To get to the graveyard.

When do zombies eat breakfast?
Just as soon as they catch you!

What sign did the zombie wear around her neck?
"Will Work for Brains."

What runs in zombie families?
Their noses.

What do you call a zombie and his ghoul friend?
A gruesome twosome.

On what day of the week do zombies cry out?
Moanday.

On what day of the week do zombies eat people?
Chewsday.

On what day of the week do zombies scare people?
Winceday.

On which day of the week do zombies drink people's bodily fluids?
Thirstday.

On which day of the week do zombies cook people?
Fryday.

What's the best way to help a starving zombie?
Give her a hand.

What do you get when you cross a zombie with a plum?
A purple people eater.

What do you get when you cross a zombie with a boy scout?
Something that scares old ladies across the street.

What do you get when you cross a zombie with a librarian?
Dead silence.

What do you get when you cross a zombie with a rose?
I don't know, but I wouldn't want to smell it.

Did you hear about the zombie hairdresser?
Each day she dyed on the job.

> Eeny meeny miny mo!
> Catch a zombie by the toe.
> If athlete's foot that toe does show,
> Then you better let it go!

How do you stop a zombie from smelling?
Cut off her nose.

What do hippie zombies say when something is really neat?
"That's ghoul, man, really ghoul!"

Where did the zombie throw the football?
Over the ghoul line.

DAD: "Why are you making faces at that zombie?"
SON: "He started it!"

What do you call a zombie door-to-door salesman?
A dead ringer.

What's black and white and red all over?
A nun being eaten by a zombie.

What do you call a dead insect?
A zom-bee.

How do they clear the ice on a zombie hockey rink?
With a Zomboni.

BOY ZOMBIE: "That pretty ghoul over there just rolled her eyes at me, and I picked them up."
GIRL ZOMBIE: "Thanks for catching my eye. I'll be keeping an eye out for you!"

favorite foods: hollow weenie, Manwich, gang greens, brain muffins, finger food, and smelt.

favorite children's toy: a deady bear.

favorite movie: The Wizard of Ooze.

favorite TV comedy show: Saturday Night Dead.

favorite football team: the Washington Deadskins.

favorite track event: the vault.

favorite brand of underwear: Zom-B.V.D.s.

favorite holiday: April Drool's Day.

favorite vacation spot: Death Valley.

favorite country: Hungary.

favorite bodies of water: the Dead Sea and the Deaditerranean.

favorite product: aftergrave lotion.

favorite jewels: tombstones.

favorite part of the military: the Marine Corpse.

favorite letter in the alphabet: G. It turns *rave* into *grave* and *rim* into *grim.*

SICKTIONARY

abdominal. referring to the stomach.

catacomb. an underground cemetery.

claustrophobia. the fear of enclosed spaces.

compliant. cooperative.

conjure. to summon up something by casting a spell.

dissension. conflict.

doppelganger. something that looks like a living person.

elude. to escape.

exorcise. to drive a spirit away from a person or place.

flotilla. a fleet of ships.

formaldehyde. a liquid used to disinfect and preserve.

goulash. a stew with meat and vegetables from Hungary.

hemoglobin. a protein in red blood cells that transports oxygen throughout the body.

hors d'ouevre. a tasty appetizer.

ire. anger.

kilt. a pleated skirt worn by Scottish men.

marinate. to soak in a tasty sauce.

necromancer. a magician, a sorcerer.

odious. hateful, disgusting.

optimistic. looking on the bright side of life.

petrified. stony, frightened.

pinion. the bony support of a wing.

poltergeist. a noisy ghost.

Ra. the Egyptian god of the sun.

sage. wise.

succulent. juicy and tasty.

Tutankhamen. A famous king of Egypt, also known as King Tut.

ALSO AVAILABLE!

SUPER FUNNY ANIMAL JOKES

RICHARD LEDERER & JIM ERTNER

WILD & WACKY ANIMAL JOKES

RICHARD LEDERER & JIM ERTNER

CLEVERLY COMICAL ANIMAL JOKES

RICHARD LEDERER & JIM ERTNER

RIP ROARING ANIMAL JOKES

RICHARD LEDERER & JIM ERTNER

ANIMAL CRACKER UPPERS JR.

RICHARD LEDERER & JIM ERTNER

Hilarious HOLIDAY Humor

Richard Lederer & Stan Kegel